W9-CUO-456

GOD'S
WAITING ROOM
OUR SPACE TO PRACTICE GODLY WAITING HABITS

DEBRA E. JOHNSON

GOD'S
WAITING ROOM

$7.95
CST
08708;1

OUR SPACE TO PRACTICE GODLY WAITING HABITS

DEBRA E. JOHNSON

248-dc22
ISBN: 1450501117
ISBN-13: 9781450501118
Library of Congress Control Number: 2010900089

PRAISE FOR GOD'S WAITING ROOM

"This book really helped me to be more aware of my thoughts and actions while waiting: whether I'm waiting in a traffic jam or for an answer to a prayer."

~ WAYNE D. BLASSINGAME

"The work is enjoyable. I believe it can give the reader a life-changing experience if the reader wants to make a change."

~ GWENDOLYN A. HAROLD
Author of *Spiritual Nutrition*

"I enjoyed the comparison of the process to the wait in the doctor's office. The pauses for reflection and prayer are great!"

~ AUDREY B. JOHNSON

"Debra has included an excellent array of scripture references for the reader to make application."

~ EVELYN KING

This work is dedicated to Jerome Johnson
who knows how to wait well.

ACKNOWLEDGEMENTS

Thanks to technical writer Thomas Tigani for his copy-editing assistance.

PREFACE

If you had asked me two weeks prior to my writing this book, I would have told you I had no intention of writing a book. Writing a book takes time, and I would have told anyone who asked me that I had no time for such an undertaking. But then my world *flipped the script*, as the slang goes. After preparing for it and waiting for it, I finally got the job I thought I wanted—and completely disliked it. Immersed in heavy sorrow and fighting off high anxiety about my future (*this would be the* third *time I was unemployed in less than two years*), I actually left that job.

Leaving the job left me with other things—primarily with the embarrassment of being unemployed again—but also with the need to *wait*.

The void that engulfed me as I waited for a new job to surface left me at my wits' end. I felt insufficient, deficient, and depressed. As the days dragged on, I was becoming deeply depressed. And I knew a deep depression was attempting to take hold of me. I, a person who normally had a bubbly disposition, didn't even want to get out of bed to start the day.

Something had to change! How was I going to mentally and spiritually survive the monotonous, long periods of waiting? *Diligently praying* to God for answers and reading sections of encouragement from Joyce Meyer's book brought about my escape from deep depression. *Praying through and living through the waiting process* taught me how to view God differently; and it also brought about the creation of this book.

I know that God will allow all who need this book to find it. So I encourage you to use the concepts and scripture passages in this book to make your waiting less painful, and prayerfully, actually enjoyable!

DEBRA E. JOHNSON
OCTOBER 2009

CONTENTS

NOTE TO THE READER:

I am making the assumption that you are a born-again Christian or at the very least that you believe that God is supreme and in charge of the world. (If you are not a born-again Christian and want to become one, see the steps to take in Appendix B - Welcome to the Idea of Salvation!) I am also assuming that you believe that Jesus Christ is the Son of God. Often, throughout this book, I give distinct roles to Jesus the Son and God the Father. I do so to keep the story flowing. I am a firm believer in the Trinity: the Father, Jesus the Son, and the Holy Spirit are one. Finally, I say very little about Satan in this book. I believe Satan influences us not to obey God in many ways, including energizing us to wait in an ungodly manner. Since I want to give Satan no glory, I rarely mention him throughout this book. I use this book instead to focus on the sovereignty and power of God to change us.

Note that scripture often says how *man* ought to do such and such. In these cases, the word *man* is a reference to mankind. So the instruction, warning, or encouragement is for women as well.

TO BEST ENJOY THIS BOOK

You must believe that:

1. **THE BIBLE IS TRUE AND WITHOUT ANY ERRORS.**

2. **GOD THE FATHER WILL HELP YOU.**

* Slow down and read the text in the Keep It Together sidebars. Practicing the truths found there helped me to keep from falling apart while I was waiting on God. I know they can help you as well.

* I have added the Create Your Own Prayer section in case, as you read this book, you want to write your own thoughts to God.

INTRODUCTION

You hate waiting! So do I! But waiting is something that we have to do all the time. Wait! Wait! Wait! Since we were tiny tots, someone, most often our parents, have told us to be patient. "Just wait," they say. "Be patient," they whisper.

Yet, we don't want to wait. All through life, as toddlers, teenagers, and even as adults, we feel that whatever it is we're waiting for should be given to us instantly. We get fretful, irritated, full of complaints, angry, and even loud if we have to wait. I once heard a preacher say that we don't like to wait because waiting messes with our minds. In the initial stages of waiting, you try to convince yourself (or at least hope) that the desired situation will soon come to past. You wait while telling yourself to be patient. Then, you wait a little longer, but as time passes, questions start to surface. Did I take all the right steps in order for the thing to happen? Did I dot all my Is and cross every T? You replay the situation in your mind and come up with a *yes*. You did all you were supposed to do—so why are you still waiting? Your mind is now all messed up because of doubt and confusion.

Waiting can also be stomach wrenching because it is a conscious reminder that we human beings control very little in our lives. Events happen to us everyday that are beyond our control. For example, upper level management decides to downsize the company or we discover we are seriously ill or we become the victim of credit card fraud or someone decides to hurt us just because he or she doesn't like the way we look or our house catches on fire or our spouse dies—the list could go on and on.

Everything in life, from little to big events, from getting over a cold, recuperating from an injury or illness, choosing which college to attend, planning a career, rearing children to become responsible adults, to ensuring that we will have a sound financial future requires waiting. If you are a good planner, you do all that you can to prepare for these events. Planning, however, does not guarantee success, and so in a large sense, we all have to wait on God to see how life pans out in the end.

You and I know that it does not reflect maturity to whine, complain, and fuss while waiting. And if you're even a little like me, you want to please God with your thoughts and your life (I John 2:28). Yet waiting is so tiring and sometimes seems downright unfair.

You don't want God to be ashamed of you at his coming. You strive everyday to live a life that is pleasing to God. You spend days or moments rehearsing snippets of sermons you've heard or scriptures you've memorized like:

Psalm 27:14

Wait on the LORD: be of good courage, and he shall strengthen thine heart: wait, I say, on the LORD.

<u>**LAMENTATIONS 3:26**</u>

It is good that a man should both hope and quietly wait for the salvation of the LORD.

And when you are having an excellent day, all day you can quote Job 14:14b "all the days of my appointed time will I wait, till my change come."

So what happens to us? The *everyday waiting* in life happens, and these scriptures just fly right out of our minds. You know you should be kind, calm, and at the very least *quiet* while waiting. But somehow while you're in the long checkout line, bank line, traffic jam, or emergency room, patience disappears while waiting.

We want to be different. If you're reading this book, then I believe that you want to not only be different but to be better. We want to be convinced that we have conquered our flesh and learned to control our souls to the glory of God the Father.

The only way I was able to find even a small amount of enjoyment in waiting was with a major attitude adjustment that began when I considered my life as time spent in a waiting room. In her book *Enjoying Where You Are on the Way to Where You Are Going*, Joyce Meyer makes a brief comment that the waiting stages or episodes along life's journey are like being in a waiting room—God's waiting room. That concept grabbed me. I have been to doctors' offices plenty of times, so I know all about being in a waiting room. What if

I really considered my waiting episodes just like the times I have to wait in a doctor's office?

A doctor's office has its own standard procedures, so God's waiting room would too. What would I find or do in God's waiting room? Join me in the discovery!

Chapter 1

ATTITUDE ADJUSTMENT

> **PROVERBS 23:7a**
>
> *For as he thinketh in his heart, so is he.*

Too often when we go to the doctor's office, we're nervous. Either we are reliving unpleasant doctor visits from the past, or we are anxious about the doctor delivering a bad report. If we replay the bad moments or expect the worst, often the circumstance will fulfill those thoughts. That's why I placed that scripture at the top of the page. Just as we connect negative thoughts with visiting the doctor, we also connect negative thoughts with waiting. If you continuously replay bad waiting experiences in your mind, more than likely you'll get more bad experiences. If you walk around thinking I hate waiting, you really will hate waiting. If you are saying to yourself I can't stand waiting, you really will not like it. Even worse, you probably won't even be standing still; you will probably be pacing back and forth or wringing your hands!

I am finding that to truly change your attitude, you must change what happens in your soul or the place of your mind, your emotions, and your will. Many of you know that humans are made up of spirit, soul, and body.

A knowledgeable Bible teacher once explained to me that the *soul is the entity of man that has to be controlled*. The spirit will follow God's leading. The body will follow whichever component is dominant. If your spirit dominates, the body will follow, and you will behave in a godly, moral manner. If your soul dominates and you normally think in carnal or self-centered ways, the body will act that out as well. Get your soul—your mind, your emotions, and your will—to think positive thoughts so that a positive attitude will gush forth.

You can then go about living scriptures such as:

➤ Yea, let none that wait on thee be ashamed (PSALM 25:3a).

➤ I waited patiently for the LORD; and he inclined unto me, and heard my cry (PSALM 40:1).

➤ I know that the Lord hath heard the voice of my supplications (PSALM 28:6).

➤ The Lord is my shepherd, I shall not want. Goodness and mercy shall follow me all the days of my life (PSALM 23:1, 6).

➤ I am blessed as I follow God and godly counselors. I shall be like a tree planted by the rivers of water

that giveth forth its fruit in its season. Whatsoever
I do, I will prosper
(PSALM 1:1-3).

➢ God will keep me from falling
(JUDE 1:24).

➢ I will trust in the Lord with all my heart. I will not
lean to my own understanding. In all my ways I will
acknowledge Him and He will direct my paths
(PROVERBS 3:5-6).

➢ I can tell God all my cares, because He cares for me
(I PETER 5:7).

➢ I know that God is for me
(PSALM 56:9).

➢ I will not condemn myself with my tongue
(MATTHEW 12:37).

➢ I will go in the path of thy commandments: for in
it I find delight
(PSALM 119:35).

➢ Greater is He that is in me than he that is in the world
(I JOHN 4:4b).

[I have paraphrased the scripture passages above.]

To further change your attitude from positive to negative, analyze the principles that are the foundation of your beliefs. To do this, I took the advice of Chuck D. Pierce of Global Harvest Ministries. In the entry for day six of his Thirty-One Day Prayer Guide for the Release of God's Provision (see http://web.ncf.ca/aj624/finances.pdf), Pierce addresses *dismantling* your unbelief. I have always struggled with completely trusting that God would always provide for me.

Here are the steps I took to change from a negative to a positive attitude. First, I charted out my needs and wants.

Things I Need	Things I Want
• Food	• Opportunities to travel
• Clothing	• Gift-buying for family and
• Shelter	friends
• Heat	• Supplies for hobbies
• Electricity	• Offering money for church
• Comprehensive health and dental Coverage and/or a belief in divine healing	• Monies for tuition and books for enrichment classes

Next I asked myself these questions:

1. WHAT DID I BELIEVE?

2. DID I BELIEVE THAT GOD WOULD PROVIDE MY NEEDS OR WANTS?

3. WOULD HE ONLY PROVIDE THEM UNDER CERTAIN CONDITIONS?

4. WHAT WORK HAD TO BE DONE ON MY PART IN ORDER FOR GOD TO PROVIDE?

I decided:

First, I had to settle within myself that God promised to provide all I needed. **Second,** He never goes back on His promises; He's incapable of lying. **Third**, I could not earn God's provision. God provides for His children because He loves us. He provides for the animals, and surely I am more precious to His heart than they. He will take care of me. **Fourth**, on days when my faith in the first through third principles falls short, I recite II Peter 1:3 "According as his divine power hath given unto us all things that *pertain* unto life and godliness, through the knowledge of him that hath called us to glory and virtue."

One more thing: we have a habit of trying to hide what our attitudes or beliefs truly are. For instance, others may think you have the proverbial patience of Job because of your outward appearance. But God the Father knows when you look calm on the outside, but you are fuming on the inside. I encourage you just to admit to God that you are not really content waiting. I am confident that you will get much further with God by just being honest.

KEEP IT TOGETHER

Are you having trouble keeping it together because you think the Father is not listening? He hears all of your prayers. In I John 5:14, we see that "He heareth us." This means He is *continually* hearing our call.

HELP ME TO WAIT PRAYERS

Dear Father:

You know I have spent many moments, many hours complaining, fussing, griping, and yelling about having to wait. Please forgive me for the negative thoughts I entertained and the ungodly behavior I displayed because I did not want to wait. I no longer want to display such behavior. Father, please help me to be transformed and renewed from the inside out. I want You to be pleased with my life. It seems hard for me to change, but I desire to change. Father, transform my thinking so that I will be new and those around me will see a new person. As I do my part by controlling my thoughts and my actions, honor me God by backing this prayer up with your power and love for me, which will help the transformation manifest itself. Thank you, Father, for seeing and hearing this heart's cry.
(CHECK OUT ROMANS 12:1-2.)

❧

Dear Father:

My soul and my emotions are trying to win over my desire to be better at waiting. You see me sitting here fretting and crying, but I don't want to

10

be sitting here fretting, crying, and not believing your Word because of what my eyes do not see. Oh Father, please give me spiritual insight as to what You are doing in my life right now. You have not abandoned me. Your Word promises me that You never leave or forsake us. Oh, Father, I am the person who is crying to You because of my troubles. You promised to save me from all my troubles. You said that while the righteous may have many afflictions, You deliver us out of them all! Please send Your comfort. Father, I stop here and receive Your comfort. I will not fall apart while I wait. My spirit will dominate. I am truly okay.

(CHECK OUT PSALM 34:6, 17, 19.)

∽

Dear Father:

Help me to truly trust that You have all of my life within Your control. If You are making me wait, You have a purpose for it. You promise that all things work together for the good of those who love You. Let not the scriptures be just words on a page that I read from time to time. Let the power behind Your Word come to life within my spirit that it might dominate over the weakness within my soul. Father, bring back to my remembrance the times when You have answered my requests in a sudden and positive manner. Let me too, remember the times that You did not allow circumstances to turn out the way I thought I wanted. How relieved I was in knowing that You gave me your unmerited favor and controlled that previous circumstance for my good and not to my hurt. Let me not abandon what I know of Your love and Your mercy just because I cannot see the answer for this current circumstance.

Your Word tells us that You freely give us all things. Therefore, if You are not freely giving me this desire, then there must be more to the circumstance than I understand. It is not in your character to make us suffer because You have nothing else to do. (**CHECK OUT ROMANS 8:28, 32.**)

༄

NO HIDING PRAYER

Dear Father:

I know You see me.

I know that Psalm 139 says, "O LORD, thou hast searched me, and known me. Thou knowest my downsitting and mine uprising, thou understandest my thought afar off. Thou compassest my path and my lying down, and art acquainted with all my ways. For there is not a word in my tongue, but, lo, O LORD, thou knowest it altogether. Thou hast beset me behind and before, and laid thine hand upon me. Such knowledge is too wonderful for me; it is high, I cannot attain unto it. Whither shall I go from thy spirit? or whither shall I flee from thy presence? If I ascend up into heaven, thou art there: if I make my bed in hell, behold, thou art there. If I take the wings of the morning, and dwell in the uttermost parts of the sea; Even there shall thy hand lead me, and thy right hand shall hold me. If I say, Surely the darkness shall cover me; even the night shall be light about me. Yea, the darkness hideth not from thee; but the night shineth as the day: the darkness and the light are both alike to thee."

Father, keep me from self-deception. Let me never believe that I can hide from You. You are everywhere.

CREATE YOUR OWN PRAYER

. . . .

. . . .

Chapter 2

THE VISIT

You get to the doctor's office, and the receptionist or nurse will invite you to be seated. (*Spiritually speaking, born-again believers can rejoice because we will be invited to sit in heaven as well. Matthew 25:34 states, "Then shall the King say unto them on his right hand, Come, ye blessed of my Father, inherit the kingdom prepared for you from the foundation of the world."*)

Once seated, you will probably be asked to fill out forms—insurance forms, health history forms, and the like.

As you know, insurance is for protection against future loss. What has been done that protects your future? Considering God the Father, He promises that He will provide for all my needs while I'm on the earth. Jesus promised to never leave or forsake me, and that I have a mansion prepared for me in heaven (Check out Philippians 4:19, Hebrews 13:5b, Matthew 28:20, and St. John 14:2.)

Next, just like you have to reflect on your health history, take a check of your personal and spiritual history. Ask yourself about your past history and your future:

➤ What positive career or personal goals have I accomplished?

➤ What career or personal goals would I like to accomplish in the next two to five years?

➤ Could I help someone achieve any of his or her goals in the next six to twelve months?

➤ What character traits could I develop so that I would be able to accomplish these goals? How good am I at being kind, faithful, diplomatic, merciful, meek, or gentle?

➤ What character traits do I need to reshape in order to accomplish my goals? Am I lazy, overbearing, harsh, or listless?

➤ How can I develop the *holiness* that I must have?

After conducting a self-evaluation, I found the one personal skill that I needed was to be able to market my skills and talents. Despite the fact that I frequently take courses and read how-to books to improve myself, I don't readily tell an employer or my network of associates about my improvements. I often say I hate job hunting, updating my resume, making business cards, or even sending out e-mails to inform others of my new accomplishments.

So here's how I started: First, I decided that telling people wasn't the problem. The problem was my anticipation of a negative response or rejection that I had learned to expect after encounters with naysayers. (Naysayers are those people who bluntly insist a thing can't be done.) Naysayers are good at making you feel that there's nothing but failure ahead for you, your idea, or the implementation of your idea. Then, I had to ask God to deliver me from the fear of rejection. Rejection comes from believing that you will not be seen *at least as* good as or better than the next person. But does not the Apostle Paul warn us against comparing ourselves to others? In II Corinthians 10:12 it is given, "For we dare not make ourselves of the number, or compare ourselves with some that commend themselves: but they measuring themselves by themselves, and comparing themselves among themselves, are not wise."

Concepts from T. Harv Eker's book *Secrets of a Millionaire Mind* crept back into my mind:

A. PEOPLE WON'T HIRE YOU IF THEY DON'T KNOW YOU EXIST.

B. PEOPLE WON'T BUY YOUR PRODUCT OR USE YOUR SERVICE IF THEY HAVE NEVER HEARD OF IT.

Second, personal experience has taught me that people usually give opportunities to people they know. Holding fast to these concepts and my experience, I worked on marketing myself. My actions and my words showed that, "I love to market myself." (Whew—at first it felt like I was lying, but I kept saying and performing the actions anyway.)

KEEP IT TOGETHER

Need to use up some wait time? Spend time in prayer. Ask God what is your purpose in this life? Write down the answers that He gives in a journal. Surprises will come from the introspection!

A fantastic way to use wait time in your life is to ask God what is your purpose. You will have to slow down your life long enough to find out the answer. It may take long stretches of days or weeks to think through the process, but it is a great investment of your time. In *Seven Habits of Highly Effective People,* Stephen R. Covey notes that too often people embark on a career, get settled in a career, even become very successful only to find out too late that they have gone up the wrong ladder. To help you in figuring out your purpose, ask yourself:

➢ What hobbies or activities do I most enjoy?

➢ Which activity that I engage in brings out my passion?

➢ What activities do I least enjoy?

➢ What would be worth dying for?

➢ What type of legacy do I want to leave behind?

An example of how I used some wait time in my life is through the writing of my life's mission statement. Six drafts later, I have:

MY LIFE'S MISSION IS

✓ To eat high-quality nutritious foods so that I maintain my mental acumen and physical abilities.

✓ To change myself first.

✓ To be a finisher of tasks, projects, and dreams.

✓ To keep my mind focused on God every day.

✓ To be honest, yet friendly to others, so that they are convinced that they have value.

✓ To extend the salvation message to someone every day.

Chapter 3

THE WAIT

DEFINITIONS FOR POOR WAITING ROOM HABITS

[These definitions have been included for the reader's convenience.
All definitions are taken from the Website www.onelook.com]

Anxious:

causing or fraught with or showing anxiety

[Note: worrying and fretting also fall into this category.]

Contentious:

having or showing a readiness to fight

Complaining:

an expression of grievance or resentment

Covetous:

wish, longing, or craving for something, especially the property of another person

Doubt:

uncertainty about the truth or factuality of existence of something; the state of being unsure of something

Envious:

showing extreme cupidity; painfully desirous of another's advantages

Murmuring:
a complaint uttered in a low and indistinct tone

DEFINITIONS FOR GOOD WAITING ROOM HABITS

[These definitions have been included for the reader's
convenience. All definitions are taken from the
Website www.onelook.com]

Faith:

a strong belief in a supernatural power or powers that
control human destiny

Gentleness:

mildness of manner or disposition

Goodness:

moral excellence or admirableness

Joy:

the emotion of great happiness

Long-suffering:

patient endurance of pain or unhappiness

Love:

any object of warm affection or devotion

Meekness:

a disposition to be patient and long-suffering; the feeling
of patient submissive humbleness

Peace:

the absence of mental stress or anxiety

Rest:
freedom from activity

(work or strain or responsibility)

Temperance:
the act of tempering

(the root word "temper"means to restrain)

Trust:
the trait of trusting; of believing in the honesty and reliability of others; certainty based on past experience

THE WAITING ROOM – POOR WAITING HABITS

> **PSALM 119:25**
> *My soul cleaveth unto the dust:*
> *quicken thou me according to thy word.*

So which of the poor waiting habits listed on pages 21-22 fit you? Do you complain, fuss, gripe, murmur, or worry? Check the calendar! When was the last time you were envious—yesterday, last week, or last month? Are you contentious, in other words, do you feel like fighting and really walloping someone? Have you gotten so worked up that you worry about an upcoming appointment? Did your worry elevate to fretting (i.e. excessive worrying)?

Look at what God's Word has to say on what we should and should not do regarding these habits!

Anxious

Philippians 4:6 Be careful for nothing; but in every thing by prayer and supplication with thanksgiving let your requests be made known unto God.

Contentious

Proverbs 21:19 *It is* better to dwell in the wilderness, than with a contentious and an angry woman.
Proverbs 26:21 *As* coals *are* to burning coals, and wood to fire; so *is* a contentious man to kindle strife.

Complaining

Lamentations 3:39-40 Wherefore doth a living man complain, a man for the punishment of his sins? Let us search and try our ways, and turn again to the LORD. (*See Appendix A for an explanation and examples of when complaining seems appropriate.*)

Covetous

Deuteronomy 5:21 Neither shalt thou desire thy neighbour's wife, neither shalt thou covet thy neighbour's house, his field, or his manservant, or his maidservant, his ox, or his ass, or any *thing* that *is* thy neighbour's.

Romans 7:7 What shall we say then? *Is* the law sin? God forbid. Nay, I had not known sin, but by the law: for I had not known lust, except the law had said, Thou shalt not covet.

Doubt

Matthew 14:28-33 And Peter answered him and said, Lord, if it be thou, bid me come unto thee on the water. And he said, Come. And when Peter was come down out of the ship, he walked on the water, to go to Jesus. But when he saw the wind boisterous, he was afraid; and beginning to sink, he cried, saying, Lord, save me. And immediately Jesus stretched forth *his* hand, and caught him, and said unto him, O thou of little faith, wherefore didst thou doubt? And when they were come into the ship, the wind ceased. Then they that were in the ship came and worshipped him, saying, Of a truth thou art the Son of God.

Matthew 21:18-22 Now in the morning as he returned into the city, he hungered. And when he saw a fig tree in the way, he came to it, and found nothing thereon, but leaves only, and said unto it, Let no fruit grow on thee henceforward for ever. And presently the fig tree withered away. And when the disciples saw *it*, they marvelled, saying, How soon is the fig tree withered away! Jesus answered and said unto them, Verily I say unto you, If ye have faith, and doubt not, ye shall not only do this *which is done* to the fig tree, but also if ye shall say unto this mountain, Be thou removed, and be thou cast into the sea; it shall be done. And all things, whatsoever ye shall ask in prayer, believing, ye shall receive.

Mark 11:23-24 For verily I say unto you, That whosoever shall say unto this mountain, Be thou removed, and be thou cast into the sea; and shall not doubt in his heart, but shall believe that those things which he saith shall come to pass; he shall have whatsoever he saith. Therefore I say unto you, What things soever ye desire, when ye pray, believe that ye receive *them,* and ye shall have *them.*

Envious

Proverbs 24:1 Be not thou envious against evil men, neither desire to be with them.

Murmuring

Numbers 14:27-29 How long *shall I bear with* this evil congregation, which murmur against me? I have heard the murmurings of the children of Israel, which they murmur against me. Say unto them, *As truly as* I live, saith the LORD, as ye have spoken in mine ears, so will I do to you: Your carcases shall fall in this wilderness; and all that were numbered of you, according to your whole number, from twenty years old and upward, which have murmured against me.

St. John 6:43-44 Jesus therefore answered and said unto them, Murmur not among yourselves. No man can come to me, except the Father which hath sent me draw him: and I will raise him up at the last day.

The Ineffectiveness of Trusting God through the Soul

All of the behaviors noted above spring from the soul. Recall that I said that the soul is your mind, emotions, and will. Our soul or the place of our emotions varies too often. One day we feel great and in good spirits. Then the slightest negative turn of events, an illness, or even a change in the weather can dampen our mood. In Psalm 25:1, 86:4, and 143:8 we see the psalmist David asking God to "lift up his soul." We, like David, need our emotions to be borne or carried by God. The inconsistency of our emotions can be too much to bear. The soul also can become wounded, bitter, and worn-out.

Wounded

Psalm 109:22 For I *am* poor and needy, and my heart is wounded within me. (In this line, the word *heart* is interchangeable with the word *soul*[1].)

Bitterness

I Samuel 1:10 And she *was* in bitterness of soul, and prayed unto the LORD, and wept sore.

Job 7:11 Therefore I will not refrain my mouth; I will speak in the anguish of my spirit; I will complain in the bitterness of my soul.

Job 21:25 And another dieth in the bitterness of his soul, and never eateth with pleasure.

Hebrews 12:15 Looking diligently lest any man fail of the grace of God; lest any root of bitterness springing up trouble *you*, and thereby many be defiled;

Worn Out

Matt. 11:28-29 Come unto me, all *ye* that labour and are heavy laden, and I will give you rest. Take my yoke upon you, and learn of me; for I am meek and lowly in heart: and ye shall find rest unto your souls.

Take note again of Psalm 25:1, Psalm 86:4, and Psalm 143:8 where man is saying to God, "I lift up my soul." God even says that our soul needs restoring and

---

1   Strong, James. *The New Strong's Expanded Exhaustive Concordance of the Bible*, (Nashville, TN: T. Nelson, 2001), Hebrew section, 58.

He graciously restores it for us. The words of Psalm 23:3 gives, "He restoreth my soul: he leadeth me in the paths of righteousness for his name's sake."

It is ineffective, maybe even unwise, to place your trust and expectations of the Father in your soul. However your spirit, that part of us that communicates with God, is not so easily swayed. Consistent prayer unto the Father allows Him to speak to our spirit that we may know His intentions and care for our lives. Our best hope for our souls is to use them to love the Lord our God. (Check out Deuteronomy 6:5.)

As I reflected on the poor waiting habits, I began to ask the Father, "God, what is it within our souls that makes us loop through these habits again and again?" Doubt became the answer, but something more than the doubt given in the section above. God gave me the idea that what really drives all of these poor waiting habits is the doubt that the Father will take care of us. Normally, we believe in the miraculous accounts of the Bible. Perhaps you believe that the Father will take care of your grandmother, your parents, your cousin, your pastor, your leader, babies, fools, or the neighbor down the lane. You say, "But He's not going to always do the best by me in every area or circumstance of my life. Yes, I have heard that He knows everything from the beginning of time to the end of time. Yes, I have heard that He is omnipresent. But that does not mean He will absolutely, positively work out all circumstances for my good. Besides, why would He help me when I have _____ (Fill in the blank with a sin) lied, cheated, committed fornication, committed adultery, murdered someone, abused drugs, been unkind, remained merciless to others, enjoyed someone else's calamity, dabbled in witchcraft, or practiced homosexuality"?

Why would He:

✓ provide for my daily needs

✓ be concerned about all that is important in my heart

✓ prepare and execute a good future for me?

Somehow, we must settle it within ourselves that the Father will let all things work together for our good. We must let the Word of God transform our minds, so that we are fully persuaded of the depth of love that the Father has for us. We must entrench ourselves in the idea that since the Father spared not his Son to die for us that there is *nothing* that is in our best interest that He won't do for us. (Check out Romans 8:28, Romans 12:2, and Romans 8:32.)

REPENTANCE PRAYER

Dear Father:

Please forgive me for the poor waiting habits I have displayed before You. I repent and turn away from the griping, fussing, complaining, murmuring, and being envious of the blessings of others. I repent of the worrying I have done as well. God, I know that I am finding it hard to wait because I want to know how this circumstance is going to end. You know how the circumstance will end. I trust that all will work out for me. I declare now to live as yours. According to Psalm 17:3, my mouth shall not transgress.

CREATE YOUR OWN PRAYER

THE WAITING ROOM – GOOD WAITING HABITS

JOB 14:14

If a man die, shall he live again? all the days of my appointed time will I wait, till my change come.

Magazines and books abound in a doctor's office; you pick one from the stack or you pull out one you brought to pass the time. Consider exercising the same behavior when you are waiting for that new job, new promotion, or improved circumstance to come along. Why not act as you do in the doctor's office? What can you do to pass the time? What new computer skill can you learn? Which professional development courses or workshops can you take in the next six to twelve months that would boost your career? Spiritually, what needs improving? Wouldn't now be an excellent time to start memorizing more scripture, preparing for next week's Sunday school lesson, or planning how to be the new Vacation Bible school director?

I thought about how I could encourage myself and you to gain good waiting habits. The nutshell answer would be *to live* the fruit of the Spirit. Just in case you haven't fully grasped what the *fruit of the Spirit* is, let me explain. The *fruit* are the character traits of the Holy Spirit that should and will operate in us if we allow the Spirit to do so. The fruit of love, joy, peace, long-suffering, gentleness, goodness, faith, meekness, and temperance (self-control) will keep us in good waiting form from now until eternity.

Love

Proverbs 10:12 Hatred stirreth up strifes: but love covereth all sins.

Romans 12:9-10 *Let* love be without dissimulation. Abhor that which is evil; cleave to that which is good. *Be* kindly affectioned one to another with brotherly love; in honour preferring one another.

Ephesians 1:15-16 Wherefore I also, after I heard of your faith in the Lord Jesus, and love unto all the saints, Cease not to give thanks for you, making mention of you in my prayers.

James 2:8 If ye fulfil the royal law according to the scripture, Thou shalt love thy neighbour as thyself, ye do well.

Joy

Psalm 16:11 Thou wilt show me the path of life: in thy presence *is* fulness of joy; at thy right hand *there are* pleasures for evermore.

St. John 15:11 These things have I spoken unto you, that my joy might remain in you, and *that* your joy might be full.

Peace

Colossians 3:15 And let the peace of God rule in your hearts, to the which also ye are called in one body; and be ye thankful.

Hebrews 12:14 Follow peace with all *men*, and holiness, without which no man shall see the Lord.

James 3:18 And the fruit of righteousness is sown in peace of them that make peace.

Long-suffering

Ephesians 4:1-2 1 Therefore, the prisoner of the Lord, beseech you that ye walk worthy of the vocation wherewith ye are called, With all lowliness and meekness, with longsuffering, forbearing one another in love.

Gentleness

Psalm 18:35 Thou hast also given me the shield of thy salvation: and thy right hand hath holden me up, and thy gentleness hath made me great.

Goodness

Romans 2:10 But glory, honour, and peace, to every man that worketh good, to the Jew first, and also to the Gentile.

Romans 15:14 And I myself also am persuaded of you, my brethren, that ye also are full of goodness, filled with all knowledge, able also to admonish one another.

Faith

Habakkuk 2:4 Behold, his soul *which* is lifted up is not upright in him: but the just shall live by his faith.

Mark 5:34 And he said unto her, Daughter, thy faith hath made thee whole; go in peace, and be whole of thy plague.

Mark 11:22 And Jesus answering saith unto them, Have faith in God.

I Corinthians 2:2-5 For I determined not to know any thing among you, save Jesus Christ, and him crucified. And I was with you in weakness, and in fear, and in much trembling. And my speech and my preaching *was* not with enticing words of man's wisdom, but in demonstration of the Spirit and of power: That your faith should not stand in the wisdom of men, but in the power of God.

Meekness

Zephaniah 2:3 Seek ye the LORD, all ye meek of the earth, which have wrought his judgment; seek righteousness, seek meekness: it may be ye shall be hid in the day of the LORD'S anger.

I Timothy 6:11 But thou, O man of God, flee these things; and follow after righteousness, godliness, faith, love, patience, meekness.

Rest

Genesis 18:3-4 And said, My Lord, if now I have found favour in thy sight, pass not away, I pray thee, from thy servant: Let a little water, I pray you, be fetched, and wash your feet, and rest yourselves under the tree.

I Kings 5:4 But now the LORD my God hath given me rest on every side, *so that there is* neither adversary nor evil occurrent.

Matthew 11:29 Take my yoke upon you, and learn of me; for I am meek and lowly in heart: and ye shall find rest unto your souls.

Acts 9:31 Then had the churches rest throughout all Judaea and Galilee and Samaria, and were edified; and walking in the fear of the Lord, and in the comfort of the Holy Ghost, were multiplied.

Temperance (Self-control)

II Peter 1:5-6 And beside this, giving all diligence, add to your faith virtue; and to virtue knowledge; And to knowledge temperance; and to temperance patience; and to patience godliness.

Trust

Psalm 4:5 Offer the sacrifices of righteousness, and put your trust in the LORD.

Isaiah 26:4 Trust ye in the LORD for ever: for in the LORD JEHOVAH *is* everlasting strength.

Nahum 1:7 The LORD *is* good, a strong hold in the day of trouble; and he knoweth them that trust in him.

II Corinthians 1:9-10 But we had the sentence of death in ourselves, that we should not trust in ourselves, but in God which raiseth the dead: Who delivered us from so great a death, and doth deliver: in whom we trust that he will yet deliver *us*.

I Timothy 4:10 For therefore we both labour and suffer reproach, because we trust in the living God, who is the Saviour of all men, specially of those that believe.

True Rest

People already know that rest involves little to no physical activity, but consider also that your mind needs rest. Take time away from those you know, the news, and newspapers. There's no way your mind can rest from worry or anxiety if you are listening to the negative economic forecasts, increasing unemployment rates, and murder and mayhem that is heaped on you through the media. Get to a quiet spot such as a park or the beach. Breathe deeply and clear your mind. Spend time in prayer talking to God. Knowing that you have connected with Him and that He has heard your prayer will swiftly bring you peace of mind.

For me, true rest means getting the house to myself and turning off the phone, so I don't even hear it ring. Then I stay in bed and do a lot of sleeping. (I like sleeping!) I take walks or write in my diary. Once I even spent a weekend at a bed and breakfast just for the purpose of resting!

Trust God's Timing

The definition given above shapes what trust is; the scriptures cited above encourage us to trust God. Let us now get to the kernel of the matter—we not only have

KEEP IT TOGETHER

Remember that one can lust over many things. Usually we associate lust with sex, but one can lust after material things and even lust over the need to control circumstances. Keep it together: pray against any lusting habits that will take you out of God's will and peace for your life.

to trust God, but more specifically we have to trust His timing.

Like me, you've probably been told often that you can't hurry God. So why do we even try? I know that sometimes when we wait, we think that God's not listening or God has forgotten us. Those thoughts should be seen as soulish. You must cancel them when they come to your mind! God does not forget! God knows the beginning of time. He knows our lives, and the earth's full history. It is stated in Ephesians 1:4 that He chose us before the foundation of the world. God knew we would be here at this point in history, and He knew the minutiae of our lives before He even spoke the world into existence. So why are we wasting our energy blaming God for what we do not see in the present and fretting about the future when we cannot control it anyway? Why be like Sarai who tried to hurry along the child that God had promised to Abram[2] by giving her handmaiden Hagar to Abram; Sarai only ended up getting sorrow for her efforts. Hagar came to despise Sarai, and God still

---

2   Sarai and Abram's names are changed to Sarah and Abraham in the seventeenth chapter of Genesis.

followed through on what He had planned. (Check out Genesis 16.)

Lust builds up in our soul, so that we get overtaken with the feeling that we cannot wait any longer and must have the object of our lust now. Here's a good reminder of the trouble lust can cause. Read on and remember the plight of the Israelites in Psalm 78:7-31.

7   That they might set their hope in God, and not forget the works of God, but keep his commandments:

8   And might not be as their fathers, a stubborn and rebellious generation; a generation *that* set not their heart aright, and whose spirit was not stedfast with God.

9   The children of Ephraim, *being* armed, *and* carrying bows, turned back in the day of battle.

10   They kept not the covenant of God, and refused to walk in his law;

11   And forgat his works, and his wonders that he had showed them.

12   Marvellous things did he in the sight of their fathers, in the land of Egypt, *in* the field of Zoan.

13   He divided the sea, and caused them to pass through; and he made the waters to stand as an heap.

14   In the daytime also he led them with a cloud, and all the night with a light of fire.

15   He clave the rocks in the wilderness, and gave *them* drink as *out of* the great depths.

16   He brought streams also out of the rock, and caused waters to run down like rivers.

¹⁷ And they sinned yet more against him by provoking the most High in the wilderness.

¹⁸ And they tempted God in their heart by asking meat for their lust.

¹⁹ Yea, they spake against God; they said, Can God furnish a table in the wilderness?

²⁰ Behold, he smote the rock, that the waters gushed out, and the streams overflowed; can he give bread also? can he provide flesh for his people?

²¹ Therefore the LORD heard *this*, and was wroth: so a fire was kindled against Jacob, and anger also came up against Israel;

²² Because they believed not in God, and trusted not in his salvation:

²³ Though he had commanded the clouds from above, and opened the doors of heaven,

²⁴ And had rained down manna upon them to eat, and had given them of the corn of heaven.

²⁵ Man did eat angels' food: he sent them meat to the full.

²⁶ He caused an east wind to blow in the heaven: and by his power he brought in the south wind.

²⁷ He rained flesh also upon them as dust, and feathered fowls like as the sand of the sea:

²⁸ And he let *it* fall in the midst of their camp, round about their habitations.

²⁹ So they did eat, and were well filled: for he gave them their own desire;

³⁰ They were not estranged from their lust. But while their meat *was* yet in their mouths,

³¹ The wrath of God came upon them, and slew the fattest of them, and smote down the chosen *men* of Israel.

As you reflect on the repercussions of lusting after a thing and learning to trust God's timing, allow me now to turn your attention to the Father's building or strengthening of your character. During my more than twenty years as a born-again Christian, I have often heard preachers say that the Father cares less about how much we cry and more about shaping our character to be more like Jesus the Son. Jesus exuded the quintessential lifestyle of being holy and human. That is, He understood human frailty without falling prey to it.

We have no such luxury, and we do not possess the internal ability to consistently remain righteous. The Apostle Paul reminds us of this in Romans 7:19 when he speaks of the good that we would do, we do not; the evil that we would not do, we end up performing it. We strive for holiness every day of our lives. To help us along, consider that God shapes us. So while you are waiting, and you think the Father is ignoring your plight, accept that His silence is significant. Consider when you are totally engaged in a hobby or in a project. Whether it is cooking, crochet, knitting, photography, painting, sculpting, fixing cars, plumbing, renovating a room, or building a website I'll bet you want silence while you're engaged in the activity. It's reasonable to say that maybe the Father and Master craftsman, too, needs some silence while working on you and me.

KEEP IT TOGETHER

Close your eyes and focus. See a new you. There you are with a more godly character. There you are practicing good waiting habits when you before would have just blown up in anger. Is it not real to you yet? Then SHHHHHH! God is working on you.

GRATEFULNESS

Just in case you are one of those people who have a hard time being quiet, open your mouth not to complain but to express gratefulness. In spite of all of our frustrating moments, disappointments, or hardships, some area of our lives has already worked out for our benefit. Write down your list and then be adventurous and share what makes you grateful.

I, Debra, am grateful for:

- ➤ My marriage of more than twenty years to a faithful spouse.
- ➤ Good health for me, my spouse, and children.
- ➤ No large student loans to repay.
- ➤ Jesus Christ being the Savior of my soul.
- ➤ Jesus Christ who will give anyone with a repentant heart another chance to do right.
- ➤ The Father, Son, and Holy Ghost, who kept my mind from unraveling, so that I did not go insane during times of great distress.
- ➤ The Father, who always sends people my way to help me when I need it most.

NOW I AM WAITING PRAYERS

Dear Father:

Hallelujah, I am learning to wait graciously and patiently. I thank you for the rest that is in my spirit, soul, and body. No longer am I pacing, complaining, fretting, or worrying about the circumstances. I thank you for the discipline I am exercising in keeping a positive attitude. I thank you that I trust that You will withhold no good thing from the righteous. Father, how blessed I am that I am learning to trust in thee. (CHECK OUT PSALM 84:11-12.)

Dear Father:

I am learning to practice godly waiting habits. Oh I am learning from Psalm 138:8 that You will perfect that which concerneth me: thy mercy, O LORD, endureth for ever: forsake not the works of thine own hands.

Dear Father:

I thank you for getting into my spirit that nothing is too hard for thee. You brought life to Sarah's dead womb when it was well beyond the stage of childbearing; You parted the Red Sea, You raised Jesus from the dead, You keep the wind in Your treasuries. Surely my circumstances are not beyond Your reach to fix. Father, oh my Father, keep my soul that I faint not. I never want to give up on You, God. I can depend on You. I speak to my soul and say, "The Father will not fail me." (CHECK OUT GENESIS 18:14, EXODUS 14:21-22, AND JEREMIAH 10:13.)

CREATE YOUR OWN PRAYER

Chapter 4

THE APPOINTMENT

In the natural, at last you get to see the doctor, and unless he or she is fatigued, your doctor wants to see you, too. He or she has a mind to help you and wants to know that you feel better. Besides, if you really enjoy that doctor's thoroughness or bedside manner, you will refer others to him or her. Seeing you turns into a plus for all concerned: you get better, and the doctor gets more patients and a thriving practice.

First, you get an opportunity to talk about your concerns. Does not the heavenly Father allow us the same privilege? (*Our Father in heaven is even better because He always hears us and is never too busy for us.*)

Isaiah 30:19 gives "For the people shall dwell in Zion at Jerusalem: thou shalt weep no more: he will be very gracious unto thee at the voice of thy cry; when he shall hear it, he will answer thee." In Lamentations 3:56-58, it is written that "Thou hast heard my voice: hide not thine ear at my breathing, at my cry. Thou drewest near in the day *that* I called upon thee: thou saidst, Fear not. O Lord, thou hast pleaded the causes of my soul; thou hast redeemed my life." Think of yourself as one of the Israelites of old while reading Isaiah 46:3-7. "Hearken unto me, O house of Jacob, and all the remnant of the house of Israel, which are borne *by me* from the belly, which are carried from the womb: And *even* to *your* old age I *am* he; and *even* to hoar hairs will I carry *you*: I have made, and I will bear; even I will carry, and will deliver *you*. To whom will ye liken me, and make *me* equal, and compare me, that we may be like? They lavish gold out of the bag, and weigh silver in the balance, *and* hire a goldsmith; and he maketh it a god: they fall down, yea, they worship. They bear him upon the shoulder, they carry him, and set him in his place, and he standeth; from his place shall he not remove: yea, *one* shall cry unto him, yet can he not answer, nor save him out of his trouble."

Second, the doctor diagnoses the condition that you have. If nothing is wrong, he or she will tell you that all is well. Almost all doctors will tell you to come back in a week, a few months, or for the next annual checkup. In the spiritual sense, God the Father will reveal to us what our condition is and how it is to be fixed. Maybe the situation will be fixed as miraculously as God parting the Red Sea for the Israelites, never allowing the three Hebrew boys in the fiery furnace to be burned to a crisp, getting enough money to pay your bills like the woman who filled all the oil pots she had obtained, or Daniel spending the night with the hungry lions that never touched him. (Check out Exodus 14:21-22, Daniel 3:27, and II Kings 4:1-7.)

Maybe God will give you favor like Joseph received. Or maybe God will encourage you to improve your character and fear not as He told Joshua after Moses had died and Gideon when he had to fight. Maybe He's asked you to make a reversal in your thinking as Saul had to do on the Damascus Road. (Check out Genesis 39:2-6, Joshua 1:8-9, Judges 6:11-16, and Acts 9:1-22.)

You must do whatever the Father tells you to do while waiting—whether it is do this, do that, or keep waiting because He knows your entire life. Jeremiah 29:11 gives us, "For I know the thoughts that I think toward you, saith the LORD, thoughts of peace, and not of evil, to give you an expected end."

However our waiting is resolved, we must rejoice! Turning our attention to the Father whose faithfulness endures to all generations will undoubtedly build our resolve to wait well.

Third, you usually have a wrap-up to your doctor visit. The office staff makes sure all your forms are filled out correctly, and then someone schedules your next visit. I liken this part of the visit spiritually to angels that minister to our needs. Just as the office staff makes sure all the paperwork is in order and digitized, so God's angels carry out God's command to protect us.

Chapter 5

EMERGENCY ROOM

II Chronicles: 29:36

And Hezekiah rejoiced, and all the people, that God had prepared the people: for the thing was done suddenly.

What about when your waiting isn't associated with a regular appointment? How do you practice godly waiting habits in the emergency room? Who could expect you to be kind, calm, and pleasant when you're overwhelmed with pain, fear, anger, misery, and death seems to mock and threaten to take you or your loved one from this side? God expects us to still remain godly. The application of the fruit of the Spirit (love, joy, peace, long-suffering gentleness, goodness, faith, self-control, and meekness) is vital in the emergency room. Take into account that He never puts more on us than we can bear, and with the emergency, He has made a way of escape for you to get through this situation.

I encourage you to repeat the scriptures or past times of deliverance that are dearest to your heart. (Once, when I passed out while doing missionary work at church, even half-dazed, I started quoting Psalm 23. It was the one scripture I could remember, and it definitely steadied my nerves so that I was not overtaken by fear.)

EMERGENCY ROOM PRAYERS

Dear Father:

Help! This is too much for me! Please give me the strength to get through this. Thank you for the people You are sending me right now to take away the pain and to help comfort me. I will not be pushy, and I will not be aggressive. I thank you, God, that I will exude poise even at a time when poise is least expected of me. Oh, praise You Father for being with me right now!

Dear Father:

I need Your help right now! Please help me! Only You can truly fix this situation. I may try to patch it up, but only You can fix it. Right now I need a quick fix. Please help because I can not get through without You. Thank you for fixing it! (Submitted by: Courtney Johnson.)

CREATE YOUR OWN PRAYER

. . . .

. . . .

Chapter 6

VICTORY

> **PHILIPPIANS 1:6**
> *Being confident of this very thing, that he which hath begun a good work in you will perform it until the day of Jesus Christ:*

On the negative, defeated side of waiting, I am sure you have moments, hours, or days of struggle. Did you find your pulse racing, chest heaving, or head throbbing? Did you feel like you were struggling between the wanting to complain and holding your tongue?

Consider the distance you've traveled, and look at how much you have changed! What's now on the other side waiting for you? Is it contentment, happiness, feelings of accomplishment, maturity, more trust in the Father, or relief? Life will always present us with challenges. Keep on waiting well. Isn't it so worth the work?

I have developed good waiting habits. Here's how I know.

_____

_____

_____

Congratulations to myself!

Signature: _____

Date: _____

Finally, the ultimate achievement is that we get to spend an eternity with the Trinity when this life is over! I Thessalonians 4:16-18 gives, "For the Lord himself shall descend from heaven with a shout, with the voice of the archangel, and with the trump of God: and the dead in Christ shall rise first: Then we which are alive *and* remain shall be caught up together with them in the clouds, to meet the Lord in the air: and so shall we ever be with the Lord. Wherefore comfort one another with these words."

I Corinthians 15:51-53 gives, "Behold, I show you a mystery; We shall not all sleep, but we shall all be changed, In a moment, in the twinkling of an eye, at the last trump: for the trumpet shall sound, and the dead shall be raised incorruptible, and we shall be changed. For this corruptible must put on incorruption, and this mortal *must* put on immortality."

Jesus the Son of God will come back to get us who are righteous.

There is no God like our God. Learning to have and to practice good waiting habits may take some work, but it will be a victorious life that we shall have and others can see. Think not of fainting as you learn to wait: for you will see the goodness of the Lord in the land of the living. And the more you shape your character to be righteous and holy, the more assured you can be that we will make it to the other side! (Check out Psalm 27:13.)

CONTENTEDLY WAITING PRAYER

Dear Father:

Thank you for showing me that I had the discipline to change where I could. Father, I thank you for allowing the Holy Spirit to rise up within me and for the scriptures that have transformed me. I used to _____

(Add your list here.)

How content, peaceful, and pleasant I now am while waiting. I can truly agree with Psalm 66:19: You, God, have listened and heeded to my prayer. I can fervently tell my friends, family, co-workers, neighbors, and the stranger to wait on You Lord. You indeed do answer prayer.

EPILOGUE

JOB 23:10

*But he knoweth the way that I take:
when he hath tried me, I shall come forth as gold.*

Three-fourths of the way through the writing of this manuscript, I kept feeling like I wasn't finished. I don't mean just putting the last chapters of the work in place—I mean more. Something was missing; something had not been accomplished within me. Most of what was on the pages, I already knew before I had the joblessness crisis that I mentioned earlier. So what had driven me to write? Yes, I needed a project to complete while waiting for another job opportunity. Yes, I wanted to share my thoughts and findings with others, so that they could also be blessed.

Nevertheless, with three-fourths of the work completed, I had not learned any new revelation about myself or God. A project such as this should bring about some type of mental maturity or spiritual growth of the author, right?

As I focused more and faced myself, I realized that I had spent this recent experience and probably much of my life seeing God through my soul or the place of my emotions and my will. I want my spirit—that part that communicates with God to be the dominant force in my life. I am tired of being in and out regarding my faith and trust in God. I don't want to be so absolutely sure of His Word, His power, and His directing of my life one moment and then wavering about it all the next.

If the writing of this book and the crisis that provoked it has finally sealed my way into walking not after the flesh but after the Spirit, I am almost ready to ask God why didn't He make all this happen sooner? I know, I know—God does all in His own time. I am exceedingly glad for the timing of God. No matter how it looks, He is *never* too late.

༄

I welcome your comments.

Send them to my email: giftedgriot@yahoo.com.

Appendix A

SOMETIMES GOD ALLOWS COMPLAINING

David, the man after God's own heart, is known for pouring his soul out to God. David sinned on a few occasions: committing adultery with Uriah's wife, Bathsheba (II Samuel 11:3-4), and counting the Israelite population before going to war instead of trusting God (I Chronicles 21:17). Yet David knew how to stay in the kindness and mercy of God. In spite of David's many instances of complaining how his enemies were out to destroy him and the trouble he lived through, David always acknowledged the sovereignty, power, majesty, and delivering capability of God.

Here is where I say God allows us to pour out our emotions to him even in a complaining manner. If we ultimately acknowledge the sovereignty, power, majesty, and delivering capability of God to resolve our situation, I believe He tolerates the complaints. (See Psalm 13, a psalm of David, and other examples below.)

Psalm 13

To the chief Musician, A Psalm of David.

1 How long wilt thou forget me, O LORD? for ever? how long wilt thou hide thy face from me?

2   How long shall I take counsel in my soul, *having* sorrow in my heart daily? how long shall mine enemy be exalted over me?

3   Consider *and* hear me, O LORD my God: lighten mine eyes, lest I sleep the *sleep of* death;

4   Lest mine enemy say, I have prevailed against him; *and* those that trouble me rejoice when I am moved.

5   But I have trusted in thy mercy; my heart shall rejoice in thy salvation.

6   I will sing unto the LORD, because he hath dealt bountifully with me.

Psalm 42

1   As the hart panteth after the water brooks, so panteth my soul after thee, O God.

2   My soul thirsteth for God, for the living God: when shall I come and appear before God?

3   My tears have been my meat day and night, while they continually say unto me, Where *is* thy God?

4   When I remember these *things*, I pour out my soul in me: for I had gone with the multitude, I went with them to the house of God, with the voice of joy and praise, with a multitude that kept holyday.

5   Why art thou cast down, O my soul? and *why* art thou disquieted in me? hope thou in God: for I shall yet praise him *for* the help of his countenance.

6   O my God, my soul is cast down within me: therefore will I remember thee from the land of Jordan, and of the Hermonites, from the hill Mizar.

7 Deep calleth unto deep at the noise of thy waterspouts: all thy waves and thy billows are gone over me.

8 *Yet* the LORD will command his lovingkindness in the daytime, and in the night his song *shall be* with me, *and* my prayer unto the God of my life.

9 I will say unto God my rock, Why hast thou forgotten me? why go I mourning because of the oppression of the enemy?

10 *As* with a sword in my bones, mine enemies reproach me; while they say daily unto me, Where *is* thy God?

11 Why art thou cast down, O my soul? and why art thou disquieted within me? hope thou in God: for I shall yet praise him, *who is* the health of my countenance, and my God.

Psalm 102:1-13

A PRAYER OF THE AFFLICTED, WHEN HE IS OVERWHELMED, AND POURETH OUT HIS COMPLAINT BEFORE THE LORD.

1 Hear my prayer, O LORD, and let my cry come unto thee.

2 Hide not thy face from me in the day *when* I am in trouble; incline thine ear unto me: in the day *when* I call answer me speedily.

3 For my days are consumed like smoke, and my bones are burned as an hearth.

4 My heart is smitten, and withered like grass; so that I forget to eat my bread.

5 By reason of the voice of my groaning my bones cleave to my skin.

6   I am like a pelican of the wilderness: I am like an owl of the desert.

7   I watch, and am as a sparrow alone upon the house top.

8   Mine enemies reproach me all the day; *and* they that are mad against me are sworn against me.

9   For I have eaten ashes like bread, and mingled my drink with weeping,

10   Because of thine indignation and thy wrath: for thou hast lifted me up, and cast me down.

11   My days *are* like a shadow that declineth; and I am withered like grass.

12   But thou, O LORD, shalt endure for ever; and thy remembrance unto all generations.

13   Thou shalt arise, *and* have mercy upon Zion: for the time to favour her, yea, the set time, is come.

Gideon, of the tribe of Manasseh, became a judge who delivered the Israelites from under the hand of Midianite oppression.

In Judges 6:11-14 you will find, "And there came an angel of the LORD, and sat under an oak which *was* in Ophrah, that *pertained* unto Joash the Abiezrite: and his son Gideon threshed wheat by the winepress, to hide *it* from the Midianites. And the angel of the LORD appeared unto him, and said unto him, The LORD *is* with thee, thou mighty man of valour. And Gideon said unto him, Oh my Lord, if the LORD be with us, why then is all this befallen us? and where *be* all his miracles which our fathers told us of, saying, Did not the LORD bring us up from Egypt? but now the LORD hath forsaken us, and delivered us into the hands of the Midianites. And the LORD looked upon him, and said, Go in this thy might, and thou shalt save Israel from the hand of the Midianites: have not I sent thee?" Judges 7:13-15 gives, "And when Gideon was come, behold, *there was* a man that told a dream unto his fellow, and said, Behold, I dreamed a dream, and, lo, a cake of barley bread tumbled into the host of Midian, and came unto a tent, and smote it that it fell, and overturned it, that the tent lay along. And his fellow answered and said, This *is* nothing else save the sword of Gideon the son of Joash, a man of Israel: *for* into his hand hath God delivered Midian, and all the host. And it was *so*, when Gideon heard the telling of the dream, and the interpretation thereof, that <u>he worshipped,</u> and returned into the host of Israel, and said, Arise; for the LORD hath delivered into your hand the host of Midian." (Emphasis added.)

Habakkuk, a minor prophet, starts in the book of Habakkuk to complain to God about the Chaldeans. Why is God allowing the Chaldeans, a people who are more wicked than the Israelites, to punish the Israelites? Does not God see? Does not God care? Yet after all of Habakkuk's woes and complaints about the injustice of it all, Habakkuk acknowledges God and his sovereignty and power. At the end of the book, in

Chapter 3:17-18, Habakkuk declares, "Although the fig tree shall not blossom, neither *shall* fruit *be* in the vines; the labour of the olive shall fail, and the fields shall yield no meat; the flock shall be cut off from the fold, and *there shall be* no herd in the stalls: Yet I will rejoice in the LORD, I will joy in the God of my salvation."

Appendix B

WELCOME TO THE IDEA OF SALVATION!

Have you heard people speak of being saved or being born-again, and you did not know what they meant? Here is a brief explanation of *being saved* or *receiving salvation*. Following the explanation are the steps you can take to become saved.

Man is made up of spirit, soul, and body. When God created us, He made us for his glory (Isaiah 43:7). Adam, the first man, had complete access to God. He fellowshipped with God: God talked with Adam, and God would even visit him in the Garden of Eden (Genesis 2).

Adam broke this fellowship or relationship when he disobeyed God and ate of the fruit that God strictly forbade him to eat. This disobedience led to his physical and spiritual death. You may ask why spiritual death? Once Adam sinned, God could no longer fellowship with Adam in the same manner because he had wrong within him. God's righteous, pure, holy, and good character (Ezra 9:15, Psalm 19:7, and Psalm 119:68) was directly opposed to the sin within Adam.

Furthermore, when Adam sinned, he passed that sinful nature down through all mankind. In Romans 5:19 it is written, "For as by one man's disobedience many were made sinners, so by the obedience of one shall many be made righteous." The first man spoken of in this verse is Adam. Adam's sin opened up the door for spiritual and physical death (Genesis 2). Now man had to physically die and spiritually die, too. The curse being spoken by God resulted in spiritual death happening instantly. Spiritual death is when a person's spirit is separated from God; physical death happened over time.

We cannot get out of physical death (Hebrews 9:27), but we can escape the curse and punishment of spiritual death. If we remain spiritually separated from God after we physically die, we cannot be with Him in heaven. We go to hell, the place God created for Satan. *By default*, those who do not believe in God's Son, Jesus Christ, go there as well. They rejected God's gift to the world—Jesus—who paid the penalty for sin.

So remember, our solution is Jesus Christ.

Jesus Christ, the Son of God, came into the world to save us from sin and its punishment, which equals being sent to eternal hell (St. John 3:16-18 and I Timothy 1:15).

Note that the second part of Romans 5:19 states that "so by the obedience of one many shall be righteous." The second man that scripture is referring to is Jesus Christ.

Jesus Christ came to save us. We, however, still must repent of our sins. Repenting of sin means that we agree with God that our behavior is wrong *and* we turn away from that behavior.

How do you get saved?
THREE STEPS TO SALVATION:

1. **ACKNOWLEDGE (SAY TO YOURSELF AND GOD) THAT YOU ARE A SINNER AND THAT YOU NEED JESUS CHRIST TO FORGIVE YOU. (ROMANS 6:7, 20-23, AND ROMANS 14:12).**
2. **BELIEVE THAT JESUS CHRIST TOOK THE PUNISHMENT FOR YOU WHEN HE DIED ON THE CROSS. (I CORINTHIANS 15:1-3).**
3. **CONFESS TO OTHERS THAT YOU ARE NOW SAVED. (ROMANS 10:9-10).**

Once you have followed these three steps, you are now saved from the punishment of your sins. You can spend eternal life in heaven with Jesus. Jesus Christ is now your personal Savior because you have personally asked Him into your life.

Welcome to God's Family!

SCRIPTURES TO USE TO HELP ASSURE YOU OF YOUR SALVATION:

St. John 3:16–18

For God so loved the world, that he gave his only begotten Son, that whosoever believeth in him should not perish, but have everlasting life. For God sent not his Son into the world to condemn the world; but that the world through him might be saved. He that believeth is not condemned but he that believeth not is condemned already, because he hath not believed on the name of the only begotten Son of God.

St. John 10:27-28

My sheep hear my voice, and I know them, and they follow me: and I give unto them eternal life; and they shall never perish, neither shall any man pluck them out of my hand.

Romans 10:13

For whosoever shall call upon the name of the Lord shall be saved.

I Corinthians 10:13

There hath no temptation taken you such as is common to man: but God is faithful, who will not suffer you to be tempted above you are able; but will with the temptation also make a way of escape that ye may be able to bear it.

I John 1:9

If we confess our sins, he is faithful to forgive us our sins, and cleanse us from all unrighteousness.

St. John 5:24

Verily, verily, I say unto you, He that heareth my word, and believeth on him that sent me, hath everlasting life, and shall not come into condemnation; but is passed from death unto life.